Transgender

Organ

Grinder

Julian Semilian

SPUITENDUIVIL

© 2002 Julian Semilian
ISBN 1-881471-90-X
Cover art and drawings: Will Alexander

Spuyten Duyvil
PO Box 1852
Cathedral Station
NYC 10025
1-800-886-5304
http://spuytenduyvil.net

A number of these poems appeared in the following magazines:
Exquisite Corpse, Syllogism, World Letter, Trepan, Arshile.

Contents

To Roger Cardinal –
Always forward; picture
slope with the imponderable!
Such a great pleasure to
make your acquaintance!
Julian Semilian
May 2002

This book is dedicated to
Will Alexander, Andrei Codrescu, and Ted Fujioka,
who pointed paths

I CREATED, BEYOND THE GLADE
LACERATED BY RIBANDS OF RARE
MUSIC, THE PHANTASM OF A FUTURE
OF NOCTURNAL LUXURY
—RIMBAUD

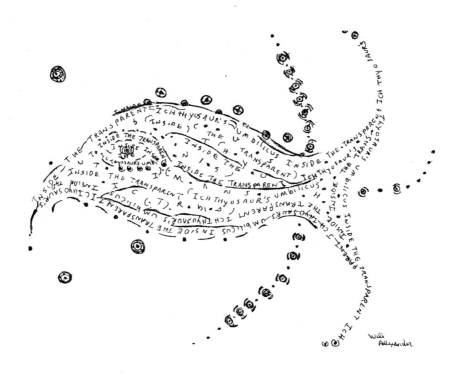

Willie
Alexander

ANNA

You are fire power, jutting jealous at the fire hose frightened of your fingernails, cerise like a ferocious predatory rose, carnivorous creature of a science of horrific observations, you have stolen my mind! It is now broken, its buses are missing, its boulevards have lost their way, I shoot out my roving finger only to find beetles and bones. And to tell you the truth, I am scared without you, where are you? Can you come and find me? I'm sliding down the back of a wind slope, saddle an obsidian sun fed steed, cool myself with a flabellum of fire, make my bed on the eyelash of a blazing willow

CONTEMPT

It is not the person we should despise but their action. I do not dare despise you because you are a human being and thus worthy of respect. Therefore when your glitter black BMW blasted past the car ahead into the oncoming lane and nearly smashed into me, it is not you I flipped my finger at, but your action. Your eyes were black and I loved you.

SAPPHIRE TURTLE BRIDE

You were the arch of triumph and your voice still makes my eyes genuflect. I persevered in my determination to lick the salt of our mutual sour cream and I preserved my eyes inside an old Dutch tobacco pouch where a few world wars had ignited, smoky willows and all, including the obligatory vacations. I fluttered my lungs and straightened my eyes and afterwards gave my life over to literature and wine; and when I came home I found you completely transformed: you were a foggy bride full of dirty teeth, splinters sticking out through them; and hardly anything was left of the mandolins which I was saving for the times when uncle Victor comes to see me and eat the pastrami which you and I bought when we bought the mournful blinding twilight rugs, the ones you adored but two days later forgot at aunt Claire's when we went there visiting her; and you swore to me that it is not true that you forgot them there because you didn't adore them anymore (which I believed) but that it had been an accident of forgetfulness which could happen to anyone; and you scolded me very harshly, yes indeed, you were a little too harsh with me that evening when you offended me deeply by calling me a freudian cretin; and you said that's why you treat me so vicious because I am so doubtful of myself and so lacking in audacity that I have a need to freudianly analyze everything to feel good about myself, shrouded up as I was in my bed-sheets of sun, and then you left with my wallet where I kept my Kansas city shoes and my eyes of tobacco ash.

ROAR

You must stop fantasizing me as a lion doing those horrible things to you, especially when your wish is to be devoured. I realize you don't really want me to devour you, it's just a fantasy to get you off, you can't help yourself — and none of us know where these fantasies come from — but still, it puts a strain on me. I want to be good, I want to be human, but when you fantasize like that I am seized, in spite of my good intentions, by a desire to rush over and do to you exactly what you fantasize; I am controlling myself for now, but if this continues to go on (and why, by the way, do you have to start fantasizing just as I am about to sit down and have dinner with my family?)— well, I can't guarantee your safety. I am not a saint — how much longer can I endure? For your own safety, you've got to know this — I can't forget just what you did to me in the past — and though I'm not a vengeful man — with you gone, I'll mourn you and all, but I think my paws will be finally healed.

THE KILLER'S APPLE

You want to know how I'm doing today? I'm feeling jumpy and suspect it is something in my heart. I reach in to find I'm right: it's wrapped in a weft of rubber bands, forming a rubber ball: if you dropped it, it would bounce. You ask: what's with the rubber bands? And what's under them? What sort of matter is it that resides under the rubber bands? I don't know. I know, it's been said that one should know oneself. Well, I who should know doesn't. I guess it is true what they say that I is another. For if I is another I is an is and not an am so don't think you're so smart crawling up here to correct my grammar. I do these lexical acrobatics like I see fit. To the right a gypsy and his bear draw a crowd. My fingers are desperately immobilized in the rubber bands. A chain link like a giant rusty earring pokes through the bear's nose. The gypsy drags the chain and the bear dances. The crowd cackles in short hysterical bursts like my neighbor Gordon when he's on the phone. My fingers glue themselves to a sticky gelatinous substance like pine resin and I can't tear them off; while you're asking me questions about my ex-wife, my heart is digesting my fingers. It feels delicious, what could be the start of my new disappearing, and I'm frightened. I must remember to bring this dichotomy up to doctor Reddick next time I see him. Perhaps it is not a heart at all but a carnivorous plant. Or who knows, even an octopus. Must have crawled into the house last night while I was talking to Gordon, then crept in while I was sleeping. Now I see that when he said pleasant dreams he meant something entirely different. I should have seen through his ruse and smacked him in the face right then and there. This virtual ocean air me cough. The night sky like tv snow! In French the Big Dipper is la Grande-Ourse, like in the poem by Rimbaud, the big bear. There is a movie on tv. The serial killer, after severing the pointing finger of a prosecutor, picks up an apple from a native fruit dish in the prosecutor's posh studio and makes off through the roof access just before the police arrives. Having taken only one bite from the apple, he places it on the red brick chimney and vanishes into the downtown smog of the metropolis. The detective follows but misses the apple. The movie unfolds without any further reference to the apple. To this day I still don't know why the apple.

AFTERNOON TEAS

oozy are the women who gloss over you!
fame, the illusion of an eclipse with blue eyes!
you figured on Sue hating you, or your ten fabulous
senses,
so you pray to the frogs, the only true source of rain,
truly very
chaste and amazed,
and like the other mother
                    super-
                              i-
                                   or,
like hairless contraltos,
like contraband cheese, you dance with your buffaloes.
and why not? living room automobiles are a cowardly
poison,
choking this morning's skiers, frightened
of their cafe latte!
or ballerinas murmuring on point,
                         on water,
because can't versify with their flutes.
a bouquet of roses is the agreeable thing then.
and the soul goes
hunting for the tyrant's appetizers, promptly exhaling
in advance:
kill this persian sun, rain dancing on arid days!

to the east the whores out on late afternoon
passes or awol remain your only rides.
they are the only visible and serene boats
in this artificial soup. an inspiration,
these queens of the sky.

TANGO

I don't wish to criticize you, but you are badly tailored: your headlights are inside out and your streetcars splay the stepmother's purple pitch. To tell you the truth, I am undone over the vapors of my circumstance and demean myself with droll anecdotes about your iron negligée. It's not that I'm delighted with this alternative: but my portion is as rigorous as the amorous affairs of a miraculous mandarin. I would have loved to holler at the emperor's hora, instead of the screech of the skylark I found inside the leeks you cooked for me with the screwdriver. But I don't wish to seem like I'm complaining: I have plenty celluloid to protect myself against the mechanism of your succulent and carnivorous sunflower; and from time to time I lose myself inside the splinters of a Moldavian rain forest. Then I squeeze like a burglar through the silk of the spiders exulted over blue fever belladonna trysts. In fact, once I made very good use of my pneuma to bash my head against the sun, and your violin. The blood flowed through your garters and the dried grapes fetched me boiling coffee full of fairy tales spun inside roosters and bulls. Yet in spite of these successes I still cast my dice over bridges overpowered by the erotic quakings of lawns observed from trains trudging though moist dusks during the time that you, do you remember? spent without me in cities where the dawn obsesses over the teeth of poisoned smoke. And I didn't want to leave you alone, or perhaps I couldn't, because you played your violin with the rivers of blood in the books I hadn't yet written. And please forgive me that I chronicle such intimacies but my gaol-keeper calling just doesn't suit me. I had dreamed of being your crab apple tree or at least some unfriendly dreadful mustard to lubricate the occult caves of your music. Perhaps this discordance was meant to teach us a dance, a crouched tango professed by the palm leaves of compassion which even the trade winds could not bend or separate from your severe and invisible crimson garter. I used a wand of red fog to startle your vaguely turbid water and I was threatened by the queen of the creeping onion shrubs, who, from way back in the feudal ages milked the cow inside the quicksand. She lit her cigar on the wagon wheel of my involuntary army and stalked me through the days I slept late so as to frighten me with fables of yet unoccupied superhighways and vampires of frail milk who were abandoned by our neighbors' autumns. Even so, she lent me tobacco and plates of spider sugar which she hatched under her armpit of silver stolen from her cinder cousins. I was grateful for these gifts which I wore proudly on my furious necktie but I wasn't sucked in by the excessive value you placed on them on the soccer fields in your blood. And as for the places where I wanted to be most: I had to sneak in, like a lithe child of flames, thief of beer and cherries; and when I was there I told you nothing about it, yet hoped that you approved and wouldn't scorn me too severely had you surprised me spitting out my mournful accordion seeds.

Cipher violin

My yearnings trained me in spit contests where I won
oranges and beer, which I carelessly tossed over the
bridges you crossed that afternoon, do you recall?
when I squandered sand on your little baby red shoes.
You whimpered and gobbled a whole donkey; then,
upon awakening, still groggy with disgust, charted for
yourself the countenance of a night owl; I easily diag-
nosed you — true to your disorder, you snorted — and
when I got home I bashed my head against the faucets
until the pigeons winged away with crimson messages
for you. You mimicked miscomprehension, and like a
stubborn ballerina of obsidian, had your little baby red
shoes messengered to me, belligerently demanding
reparation. I shook the sand off impatiently but later
shifted my drift and effortlessly dissolved them on a
moonless night (my joints intransigently enmeshed in
my notorious allure of a blue fever belladonna pitch)
then preserved them inside a trade manual I dried in
the wind, diligent daily visitor, intent on teaching me
the uses of the violin. And he didn't denounce me even
though I was lazy — so you vaunt — and my days
and years went to waste; and even now the violin is
still an amber imponderable to me but when I spit, the
wind squeezes through the beckoning of your little
baby red shoes, and howls a doleful tune, and everyone
rushes out, clapping in unison.

will alexander

PETROLEUM

Wherefore weave with toil and care
The rich robes your tyrants wear
                                    —Shelley

        The composer bows to the surg-
ing applause and introduces his new composition, a
cross pollination of Tennessee tunes and Renaissance
dances. He is popular both with the upscale downtown
classical crowd and the southern faction of the teenage
industrial goths dabbling in medieval magic and sexual
aberration rooted in Giordano Bruno's art of mnemon-
ic crowd manipulation. I make a mental note to pay
attention to the two different strains, Tennesseean and
Renaissance, and the precise mid-point of the cross-
fade, from one to the other, cowboys in tights, knights
in cowboy boots
                            the viola de gamba
scrapes across the floor like my high school history
teacher behind the barbed wire curtain, in the pre vel-
vet revolution era when she scraped her long finger-
nails on the blackboard to make us shut up and listen.
Her real name flaps helplessly in Mnemosyne's web, a
butterfly slave to its sticky tar, but her nickname flut-
ters to the surface like bat wings, Comrade Rump! She
had red curls and if you touched them they'd feel like
copper sponges. Her rump was round and tight, a pre-
Crumb Madonna rump, she was probably twenty
seven then but she's still older than me now. Her thighs
were thick, and her glittery cowboy calves, which cap-

tured me the most, so much so her shiny emerald stiletto pumps perished into the peripheral. When she revolved on heel to flash the mighty scintillating calves and chalk 1492 — 1548 on the same blackboard she clawed the instant earlier, her seams slashed us, supplicants, like sabers across the classroom, while the bristle on the calves shot out through the fabric like backlit orange barbed wire: under the microscope, forced by comrade rump to peer through when unmasked yearningly spying on the entrancing translucency of the mioritic mound behind her knees, this fabric, a vertical versus horizontal weave of braided electrical cables: there was the mound we longed to lounge on halved by the severe motherness of the sabery seam but the bars' barbed wire braided us beyond all reach o Monte Christo: the microcosm, she thrashed chastely, is no different than the macrocosm

enlarged from 5 3/8 x 2 3/4" exquisite oval miniature to be presented as amorous gift to lady love to wall size poster on socialist newsprint paper, "the Young Man Among Roses" rendered by Nicholas Hilliard, 1547 — 1619, was an enemy of the people swooning with hand to heart in white silk tights. Her crimson nail glided up his slender calves, then thighs — if he too were able to revolve in place our eyes would have feasted on his tamer but no less enticing seams as well — tapped twice on his crotch to crawl up to weak chin then suddenly shoot out like the vulture beak of class consciousness into his beady and wistful eyes: weak and effeminate, while the working classes clad in dirty burlap trousers which sagged at the knee, went about barefoot, carelessly stubbing toes, had strong well-defined chins, with clefts, powerful square jaws and large clear eyes on their soot stained sallow faces burning with yearning for revenge and revolution. Yes it is true, Comrade Rump's fingernails burned crimson with capitalist decadence, but it was only a gambit, torpedoes at the ready camouflaged as glamour fingers ever to spurt death and destruction upon the silk hosed classes — and the framed Marx, Lenin and Stalin could do nothing but beam ecstatically at the seams: she would mercilessly scout out the enemy of the people, gaze burning through whatever satin sheets he might lounge under; even in snake pit should he conceal his lacy effeminacy, she would tractor him out by his trembling tights, put him to flight, outmaneuver, overpower, subdue, subjugate and vanquish him, punish him mercilessly and continuously, hoist him and string him up with barbed wire at dawn from the highest telegraph pole as case history on display. No doubt the barbed wire would cause his hose to run, seams to bust, silk to shred, making a very bad impression on the jubilating party girls exerting themselves by day in sunny sweatshops for the sake of the sullied proletariat pausing to view and jeer on their way home to centrally heated hot water block apartments.

How their merry laughter splattered like baby blue water upon the cobblestone sidewalk! How their blood red stiletto heels clickety clacked to the beat of nationally fabricated seamed nylon, fierce fabric of a surging eastern European industrial nation, undefeatable pride of the modern toiling woman!

How their voices rang out in jubilant singing, their socialist seams long shadows dancing on the cobblestone to the beat of the oxcarts manned by dreamy rustics skillfully wielding whips on the back of their beasts from produce market to the rosy gloaming of their hillock villages so sung by the poets.

How we loved you comrade rump! how you grilled us with your copper wires when we lied! How they glittered like penalizing mirrors to better contemplate the likeness of our guilty decadence in! The tar tugging at our hearts now is our guilty love for the quicksand of your elephant thighs, your seams, comrade rump! We were your young men among roses and your copper wires of yore tore at the tights we wore for you. How we admired how you denied your silk desires! There is tar now on our tights and the Tyrannosaurus Rex of yore now turned to tar, fossil fuel to fabricate the delicate copper wire fibers of your stockings, elephant and dinosaur tightly about each other in harmonic ecstasy, oh industry! employing the "Internationale" intoning petroleum toiling proletariat engaged in the service of our yearning for you! Elephant and dinosaur lying side by side, and the translation of my memories now sprouting microsoftly on petroleum products — slithering seams across the half century to repay, so many chastisements, with chastity.

Viola de gamba, composer, now bow to the surging applause and I could slap myself for I missed the promised cross fade, from Tenesseean to Renaissance.

UNTITLED

In places concealed by the nuns I concocted occult wooden sandals out of steam; and it was in these drool places I throttled the sons of the bloody archives. And I was frightened of the roots of the steam; and I thought only of you, even when the revolutions of yearning boiled across the abyss of your mandibles; I had fought in woolen revolutions, persevered in the substructure of a melancholy mantichora; you proposed certain amorphous seasons and I believed you and released my pigeons to the shores of oppression, where ferocious step mothers eagerly awaited armed with wands of enigma and poison; all this I did, and I did it all for you. You must know this.

POETRY READING

I believe in spontaneous bewitchments.
—Antonin Artaud

I

last night at the poetry reading I was a smash!

                  the fans flung them-
selves at me, they bounded off with such abandonment
that it neared ascension to a fabulous idolatry, a tango
of such maniacal spiral soaring that I had to simply
step back not to snap. it didn't even occur to me I
should pause to confine it to the disorder of analytical
penumbra, which later marched in multi-mirrored
reverberational meditation: I was exuberant about &
free of judgment

                          the
fans, one whooshed overhead like a police helicopter &
slammed athwart into the frail body of a frenchman, a
sapsucking saprophyte of the baudrillard strain, who'd
gone on just before me, you know the sort, painting
the quarter-moon with the mane of reigning algebra
czars, for vampirically powdered post rock & roll
refuse in fishtorn nets, posturing disciple of de sade,
encroaching upon the amber of your aura with an
ecosphere of taunt, one to stun your taut ontology in
the flannel of epistemological spewage, one to aggra-
vate the mild graduates with teutonic entrancement,

one to drill them with monologues mirroring the won-
der of such condition of cogitation, impinging them
towards a future of emblematic orgiastic collectives, all
the while masticating with gusto on the intestinal aus-
terity the social sciences of seduction mimic aspiration
to without remorse

there is a type of woman I despise who flies
at that sort of frantic
creep

      mahatma of disgust & amateur in thaumatol-
ogy, I alone qualified to disbar him

a windlet stained a vein violet hissed from his skull &
flitted in the figure of eight, then flirted for locus below
— no pirouette to bedazzle me — though I am forced
to confess the left corner of my upper lip curled heav-
enward when he'd lurched into the pestilential
harangue invading a stage now memory acted by the
seductional savant blonde & her revolting invalid
sporting a wheelchair whom she'd forced to inhale a
pack of filterless camels before the stunted myrmidons,
bull-fiddle flagellants with palms glued to the benches,
yearning for the seat in the wheelchair

      but he couldn't for the life of him now
drained deform with precision, nor could he sustain
with fury, his hair was no apple impossible to paint,
more, could he cause a horse more resplendent than
light?

yet, my
peripheral fans, like most male impersonators, not
acrobats on the horse of discernment, spilled with peals
of laughter.... with glance askance, treacherous, I
spied.... my derision was rusty like fire & I mimicked
implosion like a statue of mayakovsky sight-seeing on
the horizon of disgust

         yank the wheelchairs & toss them to
those who sport them! I cackled
              like serpents wriggling
                  across the mirrored sands
                    of the
                        devotion seeking
                          unrestricted.

Then
              the spurting,
                  persistent
                  like moral abattoirs,

& suddenly
my shirt was a night lunging at my neck,
                      & suddenly
      I defined forlorn:
rameau rambunctiousness strayed elephantine!

                 & suddenly I was baited
by a fate
    of resignation to premature

propitiations!

my fans in the throws of
pealage, requested without recourse by the laughter of
fangs, maxillaries of amnesia,
a one way ticket to terrestrial travesty!

II

to wait my turn would have been mundane. I will embark!

   upon a campaign of campanology and chant like my unreasonable brothers! I shouted to shatter the salt mine mentality of my devotional drool & no sooner did I do so my fans, myopic to implications of independent origination, my fans who would be synchlipping in unison as I chanted, flirted with gravity and flung themselves at the froth of my imminent incantation,

   (— just like male impersonators I mused as I chuckled & ducked —)

   splashing against the wall & spawning abstract expressionist exquisite corpse paintings

   — the perfect equivalent of my poetry!

III

ah, the dedications of voluptuaries! A hand
for them! a hand like a swarm of flutes to grant forti-
tude at the funeral of friends, a temporary gathering at
best. but the crimson! engrossing you in the kelly-green
of the asylum where we read, now emerald, now viridi-
an, now aquamarine! porphyry quavering amidst the
adoring of cadavers! not on my knees yet with a slight
quiver I batted an iris at the amber imponderable for
conspiring to intervene. I was mingling once again at a
level where Life & Death abscond, in a blissful tango
of candelabras, on a honeymoon of seamy expecta-
tions!

in reverie I was whisked on the train by the male
impersonators as the rouged, spiked, and powdered
pubertine 17th century abyssinian ambassador to rome,
a boy enamored in jest of western baroque manner-
isms, a lash before the port authorities barged in bark-
ing at the ruffled sycophants &, before the vagabond in
the corner sneering on his concertina fictitious bewil-
derment, declared my incantations attempted honings
in the science of phantasmical forays, & thus inimical
to the quotidian masquerade. rack & pinion with
extreme prejudice, interlace in the insistence of chains,
they vamped like no longer aging mothers. yet upon
getting off the train at gettysburg, I quickly & cordially
trumpeted with unbearable buoyancy & bowed at the
parade. the vice of destiny is made of sand I quacked

                                                                I had in
fact
dined in splendor before the assembly & its ilk, a blend
of industrial magistrates in black & blind followers of
a defrocked proust, who voided all stratagem when I
voiced: death to all you who mock by approximation,
you are disbarred or under arrest! The male imperson-
ators snickered & gagged but my eyes were fixed in
derision on the restlessness of teeth of the now spin-
ning supplicants: in view of the assembly & its ilk, I
stabbed a careless finger into the amber imponderable,
which clasped it in its trumpet of early afternoon mist,
then released it to the novelty of not not. in vain they
groped for their vows, grapnels of self-distress, their
cutaways hissing with premeditation, their cutaways
wet with the history of the church, in vain they panted
for vows of ironical imams, vows, like indoctrinations
in absent-minded dropping of roses, vows, like key
desertions in armadas of moon-through-the-clouds
perusers

                                no, I'm not one to embrace the
circus — I commended myself — my stunning impa-
tience with mundane panoramas is notorious — but
when I was served with notice to join as usher, I had to
sneeze to conceal a shout

                let them in! let them in! these are the days
of the poet spy!

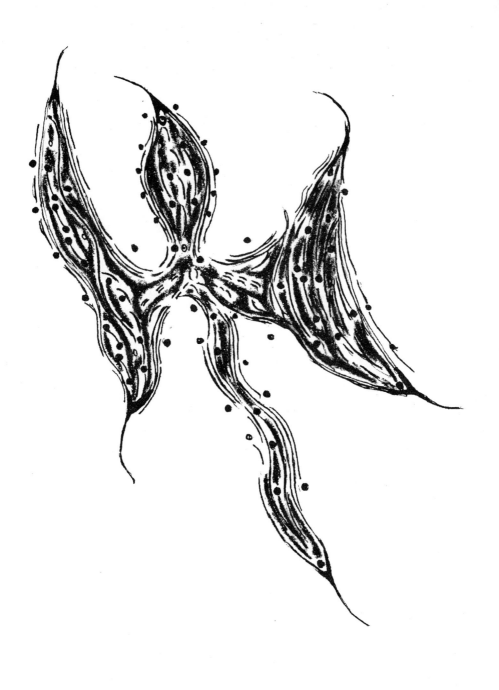

TRANSGENDER ORGAN GRINDER

I

Call me a stunning redhead, this shift. Here I am, this shift, reclaiming my charge, ensconced in oneiric osmosis with my sister Amaryllis. My sister the carnivorous Amaryllis. Watch me re-assembling my formulations, watch my carnivorous dream assemblage my sister Amaryllis embroiders me in. I am a shimmering weft of disobedient vatic intimations, having mastered in a concert of past shifts, notably as a prize in the Babylonian lottery, the tenuous task of oneiric mirroring by scent.

I have been assigned, this shift, with the task of scenting the odor of nightmares so as to metabolize them before they coagulated into the casual quotidian. Having only recently emerged from a self imposed exile to a corporate asylum for the psychically restrained, the exuberantly confined, I was still somewhat thwarted in my insurgencies by the last of a frightwork of prohibitions. Yes, a certain phantasmical restrictedness still circumscribing my personal balletics that osmosis with Amaryllis was dissolving, anthracite frightwork I acquired from the shift in this asylum, still gasping from the fumes of thwarting, this asylum honing wardens of restraint by propitiation, genuflection to mandalas of inevitability, shunting public ridicule on a shrine of restraint.

Who am I this shift? Descend into my bowels and you'll find me not; nor will you find him I consumed, him of whom I will speak; him of whom I still wish to speak; who am I this shift? Am I no more than my fitting form of imponderable emerald clarinets? Is my shimmering weft of disobedient vatic intimations, of impertinent events, the purpose of That which gave me shift? Am I peerlessly loomed with the fulgurant fingers of the Imponderable? I've peered for purposeless aeons into notions of my own essential peerlessness.

But to my purpose, this shift, prevention of a coagulating nightmare. It seems that a certain Gordo had frozen his lovely consort Andrea in the hose of submission, in the act of genuflecting in a propitiatory prie-dieux, before his posturing on a shrine to his priapic preoccupations.

Gordo was no more than an economic actor, his inner formulations were well integrated in the dogma of the feeding frenzy, yes, his inner formulations were the mandatory remedies of the day, the pale fire of pre-established September twilights was blinding to him, he was no more than a mere link in a frightwork of inter-netting fuhrers of an industry of amnesia engendering incentives, a corporate Romeo impaled by the perpetual beckoning spin of a bewitching mannequin, grafted as motivational effigy before the forced march of the common activity.

Yes, Gordo had earned his personal post on the

malady scale by grafting pre-established September twilights on Andrea's disciplinary hose, forcing her formulations to flounder in a whirling spin of abstracted lemurs, forcing her to peer incessantly into cross-eyed civets of self-contempt.

Yes, his praxis was to neutralize you by forcing you to peer into the frightwork mirror of his pre-animated definitives, to suction you into the zone of amnesia his dogmatic psychic manipulations occupied; he aspired to a posture as a fuhrer in factories for honing the propitiation techniques of the populace, hierophant of amnesia engendering incentives. To obscure this deformity he sprayed himself in azure tornado veneers and cast himself as a turbulent drama, causing his lovely consort Andrea to secrete an amber tarantula butter, but an amber from which all insurgent thought was removed, from which the Imponderable was pampered into quartered marmalade. Of this she herself could not discern.

II

Here I am riveted to my stunning aspect. Oh, my fitting form of emerald clarinets! Iridescent weft of disobedient vatic intimations! Oh my lucifer hose, obsidian shimmering within the deeper obsidian, incandescent eruptions of the vertiginous balm! Oh, the ballet of my fulgurant fingers!

I was where I no longer needed to consume myself for consuming the one who entranced me, the one I secured to my own persona, the one I left like a broken clavichord in the corner, the one I have a wish to speak of, the one I had said yes to. Yes, the one I consumed, the one I still have a wish to speak of.

Though his predilection was mantled in the imaginal vestments of a Venice Renaissance, he left the door open for an even grander solar mystery. "As I have transcended a life of economic principles", he purled, "my gesticulating is unimpeded by the mere mores of the Teutonic pedagogues of utility." He made me peer into the collection of kaleidoscopes he kept, factoried of shattered chambers of obsession, manufactured of vaguely melted maternal restraints.

Yes, his telos was a method he honed by hurling intuitional boomerangs into a unfriendly nest of absolute iguanas, through which he had transcended the institution of umbilical shackles, factory of interpretational restraints, restraints in service of the pervasive shackling of the exuberant. He hissed at ideas of fixation, spat in the face of libido arrest, painted me freely in hierophant hose, an attire which in his mirrors I adored.

He spun hypothetical cultures through hymns he intoned in praise of one's multiple spin of despised inclinations smoldering at one's core, which he perceived as the true anthracite of tumbling into sudden resorts of vatic cormorants — cormorants I might add he summoned at will — and maintained, as in a hatchery, as in a nest of restless water moccasins he'd grafted to a private sector of his obsessional ambiguity, an ululating coterie of impertinent events.

He had reduced the renaissance to an ageless mental precipitate, which he spat at his shivering adversaries, along with a general purview of the crusades, causing them to become unhinged and hurl crudely digested chunks, lingering shards of reinforced dogmas regarding the dilemma of the brooding formulations of their shifty eyed god, always plotting floods in the corner, always calculating the quantity of mercy on demeaning scales, always chewing on the forehooves of demons. This shifty eyed dog they worshipped, before the altar of quartered exuberancies, before mandalas of concrete inevitabilities, shifty eyed dog always organizing the quartering of chimeras in the corner. "I have never craved his rusty validation", he frightened them. "My formulations are an of emerald of my own redeeming. For the deviation of the sun", he touted as they cowered, "is a nightmare of circles, not the panning for gold in ostracized forests, not the beseeching of the frightwork glittering of nightmare littorals, littorals I have long been assured of."

He called me his mountain fountain, his eerie valkyrie, and promised to initiate me into his praxis of how to turn this spin of despised inclinations smoldering at my core into a full vatic opera featuring me as the murderous fravarti leading the viper retinue, baritone soprano to be worshipped in emerald clarinets by agitated crowds across the peanut galaxy. "The cruel solar flare, the day's odious conspiracy against those who dream", he declaimed as he enraptured me, and I said yes, yes, I said yes and I let him capture me in the fulguration of his firebrand fingers and leaped aimlessly to his vertiginous verb flamenco.

And yet the blinding glimmer of my emerald clarinets was like quicksand to him, was the shock of a sudden nest of water moccasins (which, blinded, he rendered as vatic cormorants.) "Chant me in your intimate anthems", he pleaded. "Make me the shadow of your peerless solar clarinets."

And I said yes, yes, and condensed the precipitate of his fierce essence in my own persona, secured his ululating coterie of disobedient events inside my own intriguing formulations; his gesticulating, so entrancing to me, — irregular balletics I so craved as my own as I craved the insurgency of his clairvoyance to spring from my chords, not his — unimpeded as it was by the mores of the teutonic pedagogues of utility, this gesticu-

lating so entrancing to me, and I undressed him of it
and embroidered it to my own core.

Yes, I said yes, and I swallowed it slowly till I felt
it shifting inside me as my very own persona, as my
ballet of disobedient iguanas, till it became my own
brand of irregular balletics.

Yes, you could say I secured him with the quick-
sand glimmer of my emerald clarinets which he adored,
yes, you could say I gave voice to the frantic chorus of
smoldering assassins at my core, assassins he released,
assassins whose intriguing formulations I followed,
followed his intriguing formulations, yes, and yet it
paralyzed me to know he became a broken clavichord
in the corner. "I will make myself the subject of
ridicule", I declaimed, craving to inflict retribution on
myself, "denounce myself before a scornful crowd."

But the paralysis lingered, and, contrary to my
nature, condemned myself to a corporate asylum for
the chimerically confined; there, to spite myself, I
charged my murderous fravarti armada smoldering at
my core with the mission to frighten the male populace
by tricking it to peer into suddenly ambiguous mirrors;
and there I multiplied myself in distress by absconding
trans-temporally with protesting pre-Baroque Venetian
baronets, yes the weather was right for trans-temporal
travel, for protesting pre-Baroque Venetian baronets,
entranced by the murderous glimmer of my emerald
clarinets, at the precise moment of the ecstatic swoon,
I, priapic fravarti in murderous emerald clarinets, and
committed sortilege by embalming them live inside my

own brand of mandala made living by their supine lowings of blinded male Juliets — here I must pause to point at shattered fragments of crusades prematurely abandoned, spontaneous acts of barbaric intrusions, erratic scrawlings of corroded bits of screaming baronets, of these I drew my new clarinets, more fierce, of these bubbled the essence of my new balletics — framed in diorama formulations of an intriguing crocodile amber, then, utmost of disobedience, intrigued the populace to insurgency by trading them, the baronet mandalas, for tickets at the Babylonian lottery.

I repelled general attacks of invasive sulphur lapping at my core by fanning myself with the delectable feather of Treason I honed when I was first initiated, do you recall? as a prize in the Babylonian lottery. That, the lottery, long before their wardens of genuflection imposed restraint by propitiation under that barbed frightwork of their shifty eyed dog they worship, always spitting his brooding formulations in the corner, always calculating the quantity of mercy on his contemptuous scales, always organizing the quartering of chimeras in the corner. Yes, not one to celebrate treaties too long, always seeking palaces ablaze with the Imponderable, I left in my place the lure of a bewitching mannequin to keep the consensus alive.

(Here I divagate to declare, I view Treason and Adoring equally, enmeshed as I am in my frightwork of blinded tarantulas, loomed with the fulgurant fingers of the Imponderable, and I balance between one and the other like the swift incandescence of a midnight fawn.)

III

So, here I am riveted to my stunning aspect. Here
I am, the baritone ballerina mantled in the imaginal
vestments of a Renaissance Venice. Here I spit in the
face of libido arrest, here I paint myself freely in hiero-
phant hose, an attire which in my mirrors I adore. Let
my shimmering weft of disobedient vatic intimations,
of impertinent events, be the purpose of That which
gave me shift. I've peered for purposeless aeons into
notions of my own essential peerlessness. Now let me
be peerlessly loomed with the fulgurant fingers of the
amber Imponderable!

IV

As I mentioned, Gordo's modus was to neutralize you by forcing you to peer into the frightwork mirror of his pre-animated definitives, to suction you into the zone of amnesia his dogmatic psychic manipulations occupied.

I could have, of course, conducted his hibernating vipers to re-arrange his definitives by suddenly intoning off key, caused the canned hurricane of his crocodiles to blow without aim; but I was afraid the prolonged nightmare diet he had placed his crocodiles on might have caused his amnesia to burst out of proportion and thus season Andrea prematurely; it wasn't my intention to smuggle her out as a burning Christian.

In oneiric osmosis with Amaryllis I devised the following ploy: through the praxis of the incantatory, to reassign the frightwork reticulation of his amnesia by shunting it to fresh venations which would cause him to act convulsively, in the manner prescribed by the poets, to lure his longings to leak out of the zone of pervasive amnesia his dogmatic psychic manipulations occupied, to trick his assemblage into rendering the shimmering yawn of Amaryllis in the purple hues of the convent of adoration Andrea had fashioned for him, transcending the entrancing September twilights of his own formulations, thus trespassing the carnivorous zone of Amaryllis while giggling in the grip of his priapic preoccupations, as though to barter them for the convulsive contraband he had secretly striven for.

"This intoning in reverse of enchanting quick-sand", I chanted, "this whirl of lucifer words I flutter in your corneas, this frightwork chorus of assassins at my core, this nest of water moccasins I've now secured you in, yes, you, you, in whose corneas I now flutter, this weft of emerald clarinets you've secretly wished me to secure you in, a sacrificial offering you've craved to make of your weft of multiple despised inclinations you've couched in amnesia, sacrificial offerings to my full vatic opera with me as your murderous fravarti, your corneas, yes, your corneas melting in sacrificial offering to this frightwork chorus of emerald assassins at my core, blinded tarantulas in the employ of tyran-nical prophecies, yes, my clarinets, blinded tarantulas in the employ of tyrannical prophecies, this vatic opera you now perceive as the flutter of my obsidian words, weft of emerald clarinets to secure you in, nest of water moccasins you've wished to be secured in in sacrificial offering, and you said yes, yes, my emerald obsidian corneas, witnesses to your soft dying..."

I needed to chant no longer: he felt himself crav-ing to mimick the forced morphallaxis of phantoms. "I have always longed to balance on the soft shoulders of glow-worms", he giggled convulsively as he flung his frame into Amaryllis's yawn and diaphanously meta-morphosed into the protoplasmic jet of her lavender metabolical rage.

I peered at Andrea. Her hose of submission had suddenly transmuted into the alabaster balletics of re-

released vatic iguanas! Her formulations no longer intoning hymns to the civets of self contempt. "I will order statues to your frightworks to be chiseled in Emerald Imponderable", she shouted and leaped. She was suddenly entrancing, like perusing into peerless solar clarinets. Their luminous spill made me rash and I shot out my fulgurant fingers — o the ballet of my ful-gurant fingers! I, priapic fravarti, riveted as I was to their luminous spill! Architecture of peerless soprano celestinas!

No, I was not about to examine the translucence of limbs under the moral microscope, as momentary self entrancement was my purpose, come what may...

Julian Semilian is a poet, novelist and essayist who teaches film editing at the North Carolina School of the Arts, after 24 years in Hollywood as a film editor. His poems, translations and essays have appeared in *Exquisite Corpse, Syllogism, World Letter, Arshile, Callaloo, Trepan, Mr. Knife and Miss Fork, Urvox, Transcendental Friend, Xavier*. His serial, *The Skeuromorph Detective*, appears regularly in the *Exquisite Corpse*. His translations of Paul Celan's Romanian poems will be out this year from Green Integer.

S P U Y T E N   D U Y V I L